INTERNET PASSWORD JOURNAL

ROCK
POINT

QUARTOKNOWS.COM
NEW YORK, NY

Brimming with creative inspiration, how-to projects, and useful information to enrich your everyday life, Quarto Knows is a favorite destination for those pursuing their interests and passions. Visit our site and dig deeper with our books into your area of interest: Quarto Creates, Quarto Cooks, Quarto Homes, Quarto Lives, Quarto Drives, Quarto Explores, Quarto Gifts, or Quarto Kids.

© 2018 Quarto Publishing Group USA Inc.

First published in 2018 by Rock Point,
an imprint of The Quarto Group
142 West 36th Street, 4th Floor
New York, NY 10018 USA
T (212) 779-4972 F (212) 779-6058
www.QuartoKnows.com

Rock Point titles are also available at discount for retail, wholesale, promotional, and bulk purchase. For details, contact the Special Sales Manager by email at specialsales@quarto.com or by mail at The Quarto Group, Attn: Special Sales Manager, 100 Cummings Center, Suite 265D, Beverly, MA 01915, USA.

10 9 8 7 6 5 4

ISBN: 978-1-63106-566-8

Editorial Director: Rage Kindelsperger
Managing Editor: Erin Canning
Cover and Interior Design: Kate Smith
Design Manager: Phil Buchanan

Printed in China

INTRODUCTION
Stop! *Please read the following.*

This *Internet Password Journal* was created to make your life easier by giving you a way to organize and record the endless and ever-changing usernames, passwords, security questions, and web addresses that are an integral part of your everyday life.

This book is organized into four sections to store your information: website usernames and passwords, software license information, wireless network settings, and notes. With these, you can keep all your web and software information in one place, so you won't have to dig through paperwork or old e-mails the next time your computer asks you for a 16-digit password you've totally forgotten about.

But before you begin, take a moment to read the following Internet safety tips on how to construct usernames and passwords that will be secure.

INTERNET PASSWORD SAFETY AND NAMING TIPS

It's very tempting to create login names and passwords that are easy to remember, or to use the same password for multiple accounts. But in the digital age, that's just asking for trouble. Hackers have developed password-cracking software that can endlessly run thousands of options—until they find the right combination. The weaker your password—using real words or names associated with your accounts (especially anything posted to social media sites), reusing passwords, creating short logins or password names—the more likely it is for hackers to crack your code.

Thankfully, with this book, you no longer need to settle for simple passwords. With our hacker-proof password tips, recommended by security experts, you can create elaborate and secure passwords that you can keep safely stored in this book.

But secure passwords alone aren't enough to keep your private information safe. Follow the tips in the next section, *Keeping Logins and Passwords Safe*, to further protect your online identity.

HOW TO CREATE HACKER-PROOF LOGINS AND PASSWORDS
Tips for making your logins and passwords hacker-proof:

- **The longer the name, the harder it is to crack.** Experts recommend that logins and/or passwords be at least 8 characters in length (some sites have a minimum number of required characters, but even if the required number is small, aim for more than the minimum). The longer your password, the harder it is to crack.
- **Use a combination of uppercase and lowercase letters, characters, numbers, and symbols.** Avoid using all letters or all numbers, as these combinations can be easy to decipher using common-sense tactics.

- **Use a random approach (literally random) or a system that only you would know.** For example, substitute symbols for letters—replace "A" with @, or "S" with $.
- **Absolutely do not use Social Security numbers, phone numbers, or birthdays.** All of these are considered vulnerable. So are things that are "known" about you, such as a license plate number, or your date of graduation or marriage. Come up with something completely new.
- **Don't use proper names.** This means you, your spouse, your kids, or your pets.
- **Try not to use any word that can be found in the dictionary (not even foreign words or phrases).** A nonsense word you like works best. Slang is a good substitution for normal words.
- **Do not use the same word in your password as your username.** Make them as wildly different as possible.
- **Avoid "logical" combinations, such as "ABC" or "123" in the string.** You'd be surprised how many people do this.
- **Change your logins and passwords—often.** This can be frustrating, yes, but it's worth it. And anyway, remembering new passwords is what this book is for!
- **Avoid re-using a login or password.** Use something new, every time.
- **If the site analyzes the "strength" of your password, make sure your password meets the strongest indication.** Because why not be as secure as possible?

Here are a couple of examples of smart password habits:

- **Select a word, spell it backward, and insert numbers and/or symbols.** For example, "street" spelled backward is "teerts"—you could incorporate your street name and address. (Don't do this if your address actually includes the word "street." Use another word.) Let's say you use the first two letters of the word spelled backward, then the first number of your address, then two letters of your actual street address. Then repeat (but avoid spelling an actual word). So, for example, if your address is 410 River Road, try "te4Rier1vetsOrR."

- **Use mnemonic devices.** For example, think of a phrase (maybe it's a song title, maybe it's a line from a book), and use the first letter from each word. Throw in some uppercase letters, numbers, and symbols for good measure. Here's an example: "It was the best of times, it was the worst of times" = "iwtbotiwtwot." But wait, you're not done. *A Tale of Two Cities*, by Charles Dickens, from which this quote came, was written in 1859. So maybe it becomes, "iwtC9bot5iwtD8wot1#"—and there you have a 19-character login or password.

Some experts say it's not *if*, but *when* your security will be breached.

KEEPING LOGINS AND PASSWORDS SAFE

Once you've created some hard-to-crack passwords, you need to safeguard your passwords and logins. Some tips to remember include:

- Do not log in to secure sites at potentially dangerous Wi-Fi locations (the airport, coffee shops, and Internet cafes, for example).
- Never email your login or password to another person.
- Do not tell anyone your logins or passwords, not even your best friend. They may not always be your friend.
- Keep this *Internet Password Journal* in a secure location that only you know. It's as valuable as your passport.
- Change your login or password often (we say this twice for a reason).

- Take advantage of a site offering a series of password security questions; some even let you write the question. But don't answer it logically; use a response that only you would know. If the site's security question is "Your mother's maiden name," then set the "answer" as a favorite song title.
- Maintain an overall Internet security system to guard against malware.
- Use a different login/password for every account.
- Be cautious about the amount and type of information you put on social media; all of it can be used by hackers to gain information about you.

REMEMBER
Be diligent with your online accounts.
Hackers, scammers, and identity thieves are everywhere, and by following the tips in this book, you can make it harder for them to gain access to your online accounts and passwords.

This is extremely sensitive information. Keep it in a safe and secure location, preferably one that only you know. Do not travel with this book. It is as valuable as a passport, and should be treated as carefully.

*Important Note: the publisher of this book cannot be held responsible or liable for any damages, errors, consequences, or losses that may result from any user recording and storing data in this book.

ONE MORE TIME—REMEMBER:

- Use a combination of letters, numbers, and symbols.

- The longer your passwords are, the harder they are to crack.

- Do not tell anyone your logins or passwords. No one. Not a soul.

- Change your passwords often.

WEBSITE

Username:

Date/Password:

Date/Password:

Date/Password:

Date/Password:

Date/Password:

WEBSITE

Username:

Date/Password:

Date/Password:

Date/Password:

Date/Password:

Date/Password:

WEBSITE

Username:

Date/Password:

Date/Password:

Date/Password:

Date/Password:

Date/Password:

WEBSITE

Username:

Date/Password:

Date/Password:

Date/Password:

Date/Password:

Date/Password:

WEBSITE

Username:

Date/Password:

Date/Password:

Date/Password:

Date/Password:

Date/Password:

WEBSITE

Username:

Date/Password:

Date/Password:

Date/Password:

Date/Password:

Date/Password:

WEBSITE

Username:

Date/Password:

Date/Password:

Date/Password:

Date/Password:

Date/Password:

WEBSITE

Username:

Date/Password:

Date/Password:

Date/Password:

Date/Password:

Date/Password:

WEBSITE

Username:

Date/Password:

Date/Password:

Date/Password:

Date/Password:

Date/Password:

WEBSITE

Username:

Date/Password:

Date/Password:

Date/Password:

Date/Password:

Date/Password:

WEBSITE

Username:

Date/Password:

Date/Password:

Date/Password:

Date/Password:

Date/Password:

WEBSITE

Username:

Date/Password:

Date/Password:

Date/Password:

Date/Password:

Date/Password:

WEBSITE

Username:

Date/Password:

Date/Password:

Date/Password:

Date/Password:

Date/Password:

WEBSITE

Username:

Date/Password:

Date/Password:

Date/Password:

Date/Password:

Date/Password:

WEBSITE

Username:

Date/Password:

Date/Password:

Date/Password:

Date/Password:

Date/Password:

WEBSITE

Username:

Date/Password:

Date/Password:

Date/Password:

Date/Password:

Date/Password:

WEBSITE

Username:

Date/Password:

Date/Password:

Date/Password:

Date/Password:

Date/Password:

WEBSITE

Username:

Date/Password:

Date/Password:

Date/Password:

Date/Password:

Date/Password:

WEBSITE

Username:

Date/Password:

Date/Password:

Date/Password:

Date/Password:

Date/Password:

WEBSITE

Username:

Date/Password:

Date/Password:

Date/Password:

Date/Password:

Date/Password:

WEBSITE

Username:

Date/Password:

Date/Password:

Date/Password:

Date/Password:

Date/Password:

WEBSITE

Username:

Date/Password:

Date/Password:

Date/Password:

Date/Password:

Date/Password:

WEBSITE

Username:

Date/Password:

Date/Password:

Date/Password:

Date/Password:

Date/Password:

WEBSITE

Username:

Date/Password:

Date/Password:

Date/Password:

Date/Password:

Date/Password:

WEBSITE

Username:

Date/Password:

Date/Password:

Date/Password:

Date/Password:

Date/Password:

WEBSITE

Username:

Date/Password:

Date/Password:

Date/Password:

Date/Password:

Date/Password:

WEBSITE

Username:

Date/Password:

Date/Password:

Date/Password:

Date/Password:

Date/Password:

WEBSITE

Username:

Date/Password:

Date/Password:

Date/Password:

Date/Password:

Date/Password:

WEBSITE

Username:

Date/Password:

Date/Password:

Date/Password:

Date/Password:

Date/Password:

WEBSITE

Username:

Date/Password:

Date/Password:

Date/Password:

Date/Password:

Date/Password:

WEBSITE

Username:

Date/Password:

Date/Password:

Date/Password:

Date/Password:

Date/Password:

WEBSITE

Username:

Date/Password:

Date/Password:

Date/Password:

Date/Password:

Date/Password:

WEBSITE

Username:

Date/Password:

Date/Password:

Date/Password:

Date/Password:

Date/Password:

WEBSITE

Username:

Date/Password:

Date/Password:

Date/Password:

Date/Password:

Date/Password:

WEBSITE

Username:

Date/Password:

Date/Password:

Date/Password:

Date/Password:

Date/Password:

WEBSITE

Username:

Date/Password:

Date/Password:

Date/Password:

Date/Password:

Date/Password:

WEBSITE

Username:

Date/Password:

Date/Password:

Date/Password:

Date/Password:

Date/Password:

WEBSITE

Username:

Date/Password:

Date/Password:

Date/Password:

Date/Password:

Date/Password:

WEBSITE

Username:

Date/Password:

Date/Password:

Date/Password:

Date/Password:

Date/Password:

WEBSITE

Username:

Date/Password:

Date/Password:

Date/Password:

Date/Password:

Date/Password:

WEBSITE

Username:

Date/Password:

Date/Password:

Date/Password:

Date/Password:

Date/Password:

WEBSITE

Username:

Date/Password:

Date/Password:

Date/Password:

Date/Password:

Date/Password:

WEBSITE

Username:

Date/Password:

Date/Password:

Date/Password:

Date/Password:

Date/Password:

WEBSITE

Username:

Date/Password:

Date/Password:

Date/Password:

Date/Password:

Date/Password:

WEBSITE

Username:

Date/Password:

Date/Password:

Date/Password:

Date/Password:

Date/Password:

WEBSITE

Username:

Date/Password:

Date/Password:

Date/Password:

Date/Password:

Date/Password:

WEBSITE

Username:

Date/Password:

Date/Password:

Date/Password:

Date/Password:

Date/Password:

WEBSITE

Username:

Date/Password:

Date/Password:

Date/Password:

Date/Password:

Date/Password:

WEBSITE

Username:

Date/Password:

Date/Password:

Date/Password:

Date/Password:

Date/Password:

WEBSITE

Username:

Date/Password:

Date/Password:

Date/Password:

Date/Password:

Date/Password:

WEBSITE

Username:

Date/Password:

Date/Password:

Date/Password:

Date/Password:

Date/Password:

WEBSITE

Username:

Date/Password:

Date/Password:

Date/Password:

Date/Password:

Date/Password:

WEBSITE

Username:

Date/Password:

Date/Password:

Date/Password:

Date/Password:

Date/Password:

WEBSITE

Username:

Date/Password:

Date/Password:

Date/Password:

Date/Password:

Date/Password:

WEBSITE

Username:

Date/Password:

Date/Password:

Date/Password:

Date/Password:

Date/Password:

WEBSITE

Username:

Date/Password:

Date/Password:

Date/Password:

Date/Password:

Date/Password:

WEBSITE

Username:

Date/Password:

Date/Password:

Date/Password:

Date/Password:

Date/Password:

WEBSITE

Username:

Date/Password:

Date/Password:

Date/Password:

Date/Password:

Date/Password:

WEBSITE

Username:

Date/Password:

Date/Password:

Date/Password:

Date/Password:

Date/Password:

WEBSITE

Username:

Date/Password:

Date/Password:

Date/Password:

Date/Password:

Date/Password:

WEBSITE

Username:

Date/Password:

Date/Password:

Date/Password:

Date/Password:

Date/Password:

WEBSITE

Username:

Date/Password:

Date/Password:

Date/Password:

Date/Password:

Date/Password:

WEBSITE

Username:

Date/Password:

Date/Password:

Date/Password:

Date/Password:

Date/Password:

WEBSITE

Username:

Date/Password:

Date/Password:

Date/Password:

Date/Password:

Date/Password:

WEBSITE

Username:

Date/Password:

Date/Password:

Date/Password:

Date/Password:

Date/Password:

WEBSITE

Username:

Date/Password:

Date/Password:

Date/Password:

Date/Password:

Date/Password:

WEBSITE

Username:

Date/Password:

Date/Password:

Date/Password:

Date/Password:

Date/Password:

WEBSITE

Username:

Date/Password:

Date/Password:

Date/Password:

Date/Password:

Date/Password:

WEBSITE

Username:

Date/Password:

Date/Password:

Date/Password:

Date/Password:

Date/Password:

WEBSITE

Username:

Date/Password:

Date/Password:

Date/Password:

Date/Password:

Date/Password:

WEBSITE

Username:

Date/Password:

Date/Password:

Date/Password:

Date/Password:

Date/Password:

WEBSITE

Username:

Date/Password:

Date/Password:

Date/Password:

Date/Password:

Date/Password:

WEBSITE

Username:

Date/Password:

Date/Password:

Date/Password:

Date/Password:

Date/Password:

G
H

WEBSITE

Username:

Date/Password:

Date/Password:

Date/Password:

Date/Password:

Date/Password:

WEBSITE

Username:

Date/Password:

Date/Password:

Date/Password:

Date/Password:

Date/Password:

WEBSITE

Username:

Date/Password:

Date/Password:

Date/Password:

Date/Password:

Date/Password:

WEBSITE

Username:

Date/Password:

Date/Password:

Date/Password:

Date/Password:

Date/Password:

WEBSITE

Username:

Date/Password:

Date/Password:

Date/Password:

Date/Password:

Date/Password:

WEBSITE

Username:

Date/Password:

Date/Password:

Date/Password:

Date/Password:

Date/Password:

G
H

WEBSITE

Username:

Date/Password:

Date/Password:

Date/Password:

Date/Password:

Date/Password:

WEBSITE

Username:

Date/Password:

Date/Password:

Date/Password:

Date/Password:

Date/Password:

WEBSITE

Username:

Date/Password:

Date/Password:

Date/Password:

Date/Password:

Date/Password:

WEBSITE

Username:

Date/Password:

Date/Password:

Date/Password:

Date/Password:

Date/Password:

WEBSITE

Username:

Date/Password:

Date/Password:

Date/Password:

Date/Password:

Date/Password:

WEBSITE

Username:

Date/Password:

Date/Password:

Date/Password:

Date/Password:

Date/Password:

G
H

WEBSITE

Username:

Date/Password:

Date/Password:

Date/Password:

Date/Password:

Date/Password:

WEBSITE

Username:

Date/Password:

Date/Password:

Date/Password:

Date/Password:

Date/Password:

WEBSITE

Username:

Date/Password:

Date/Password:

Date/Password:

Date/Password:

Date/Password:

WEBSITE

Username:

Date/Password:

Date/Password:

Date/Password:

Date/Password:

Date/Password:

WEBSITE

Username:

Date/Password:

Date/Password:

Date/Password:

Date/Password:

Date/Password:

WEBSITE

Username:

Date/Password:

Date/Password:

Date/Password:

Date/Password:

Date/Password:

WEBSITE

Username:

Date/Password:

Date/Password:

Date/Password:

Date/Password:

Date/Password:

WEBSITE

Username:

Date/Password:

Date/Password:

Date/Password:

Date/Password:

Date/Password:

G
H

WEBSITE

Username:

Date/Password:

Date/Password:

Date/Password:

Date/Password:

Date/Password:

WEBSITE

Username:

Date/Password:

Date/Password:

Date/Password:

Date/Password:

Date/Password:

WEBSITE

Username:

Date/Password:

Date/Password:

Date/Password:

Date/Password:

Date/Password:

WEBSITE

Username:

Date/Password:

Date/Password:

Date/Password:

Date/Password:

Date/Password:

I
J

WEBSITE

Username:

Date/Password:

Date/Password:

Date/Password:

Date/Password:

Date/Password:

WEBSITE

Username:

Date/Password:

Date/Password:

Date/Password:

Date/Password:

Date/Password:

WEBSITE

Username:

Date/Password:

Date/Password:

Date/Password:

Date/Password:

Date/Password:

WEBSITE

Username:

Date/Password:

Date/Password:

Date/Password:

Date/Password:

Date/Password:

WEBSITE

Username:

Date/Password:

Date/Password:

Date/Password:

Date/Password:

Date/Password:

WEBSITE

Username:

Date/Password:

Date/Password:

Date/Password:

Date/Password:

Date/Password:

WEBSITE

Username:

Date/Password:

Date/Password:

Date/Password:

Date/Password:

Date/Password:

WEBSITE

Username:

Date/Password:

Date/Password:

Date/Password:

Date/Password:

Date/Password:

WEBSITE

Username:

Date/Password:

Date/Password:

Date/Password:

Date/Password:

Date/Password:

WEBSITE

Username:

Date/Password:

Date/Password:

Date/Password:

Date/Password:

Date/Password:

WEBSITE

Username:

Date/Password:

Date/Password:

Date/Password:

Date/Password:

Date/Password:

WEBSITE

Username:

Date/Password:

Date/Password:

Date/Password:

Date/Password:

Date/Password:

WEBSITE

Username:

Date/Password:

Date/Password:

Date/Password:

Date/Password:

Date/Password:

WEBSITE

Username:

Date/Password:

Date/Password:

Date/Password:

Date/Password:

Date/Password:

WEBSITE

Username:

Date/Password:

Date/Password:

Date/Password:

Date/Password:

Date/Password:

WEBSITE

Username:

Date/Password:

Date/Password:

Date/Password:

Date/Password:

Date/Password:

WEBSITE

Username:

Date/Password:

Date/Password:

Date/Password:

Date/Password:

Date/Password:

WEBSITE

Username:

Date/Password:

Date/Password:

Date/Password:

Date/Password:

Date/Password:

WEBSITE

Username:

Date/Password:

Date/Password:

Date/Password:

Date/Password:

Date/Password:

WEBSITE

Username:

Date/Password:

Date/Password:

Date/Password:

Date/Password:

Date/Password:

WEBSITE

Username:

Date/Password:

Date/Password:

Date/Password:

Date/Password:

Date/Password:

WEBSITE

Username:

Date/Password:

Date/Password:

Date/Password:

Date/Password:

Date/Password:

WEBSITE

Username:

Date/Password:

Date/Password:

Date/Password:

Date/Password:

Date/Password:

WEBSITE

Username:

Date/Password:

Date/Password:

Date/Password:

Date/Password:

Date/Password:

WEBSITE

Username:

Date/Password:

Date/Password:

Date/Password:

Date/Password:

Date/Password:

WEBSITE

Username:

Date/Password:

Date/Password:

Date/Password:

Date/Password:

Date/Password:

WEBSITE

Username:

Date/Password:

Date/Password:

Date/Password:

Date/Password:

Date/Password:

WEBSITE

Username:

Date/Password:

Date/Password:

Date/Password:

Date/Password:

Date/Password:

WEBSITE

Username:

Date/Password:

Date/Password:

Date/Password:

Date/Password:

Date/Password:

WEBSITE

Username:

Date/Password:

Date/Password:

Date/Password:

Date/Password:

Date/Password:

WEBSITE

Username:

Date/Password:

Date/Password:

Date/Password:

Date/Password:

Date/Password:

WEBSITE

Username:

Date/Password:

Date/Password:

Date/Password:

Date/Password:

Date/Password:

WEBSITE

Username:

Date/Password:

Date/Password:

Date/Password:

Date/Password:

Date/Password:

WEBSITE

Username:

Date/Password:

Date/Password:

Date/Password:

Date/Password:

Date/Password:

WEBSITE

Username:

Date/Password:

Date/Password:

Date/Password:

Date/Password:

Date/Password:

WEBSITE

Username:

Date/Password:

Date/Password:

Date/Password:

Date/Password:

Date/Password:

WEBSITE

Username:

Date/Password:

Date/Password:

Date/Password:

Date/Password:

Date/Password:

WEBSITE

Username:

Date/Password:

Date/Password:

Date/Password:

Date/Password:

Date/Password:

K
L

WEBSITE

Username:

Date/Password:

Date/Password:

Date/Password:

Date/Password:

Date/Password:

WEBSITE

Username:

Date/Password:

Date/Password:

Date/Password:

Date/Password:

Date/Password:

WEBSITE

Username:

Date/Password:

Date/Password:

Date/Password:

Date/Password:

Date/Password:

WEBSITE

Username:

Date/Password:

Date/Password:

Date/Password:

Date/Password:

Date/Password:

WEBSITE

Username:

Date/Password:

Date/Password:

Date/Password:

Date/Password:

Date/Password:

WEBSITE

Username:

Date/Password:

Date/Password:

Date/Password:

Date/Password:

Date/Password:

K
L

WEBSITE

Username:

Date/Password:

Date/Password:

Date/Password:

Date/Password:

Date/Password:

WEBSITE

Username:

Date/Password:

Date/Password:

Date/Password:

Date/Password:

Date/Password:

WEBSITE

Username:

Date/Password:

Date/Password:

Date/Password:

Date/Password:

Date/Password:

WEBSITE

Username:

Date/Password:

Date/Password:

Date/Password:

Date/Password:

Date/Password:

WEBSITE

Username:

Date/Password:

Date/Password:

Date/Password:

Date/Password:

Date/Password:

WEBSITE

Username:

Date/Password:

Date/Password:

Date/Password:

Date/Password:

Date/Password:

M
N

WEBSITE

Username:

Date/Password:

Date/Password:

Date/Password:

Date/Password:

Date/Password:

WEBSITE

Username:

Date/Password:

Date/Password:

Date/Password:

Date/Password:

Date/Password:

WEBSITE

Username:

Date/Password:

Date/Password:

Date/Password:

Date/Password:

Date/Password:

WEBSITE

Username:

Date/Password:

Date/Password:

Date/Password:

Date/Password:

Date/Password:

WEBSITE

Username:

Date/Password:

Date/Password:

Date/Password:

Date/Password:

Date/Password:

WEBSITE

Username:

Date/Password:

Date/Password:

Date/Password:

Date/Password:

Date/Password:

WEBSITE

Username:

Date/Password:

Date/Password:

Date/Password:

Date/Password:

Date/Password:

WEBSITE

Username:

Date/Password:

Date/Password:

Date/Password:

Date/Password:

Date/Password:

WEBSITE

Username:

Date/Password:

Date/Password:

Date/Password:

Date/Password:

Date/Password:

WEBSITE

Username:

Date/Password:

Date/Password:

Date/Password:

Date/Password:

Date/Password:

WEBSITE

Username:

Date/Password:

Date/Password:

Date/Password:

Date/Password:

Date/Password:

WEBSITE

Username:

Date/Password:

Date/Password:

Date/Password:

Date/Password:

Date/Password:

WEBSITE

Username:

Date/Password:

Date/Password:

Date/Password:

Date/Password:

Date/Password:

WEBSITE

Username:

Date/Password:

Date/Password:

Date/Password:

Date/Password:

Date/Password:

WEBSITE

Username:

Date/Password:

Date/Password:

Date/Password:

Date/Password:

Date/Password:

WEBSITE

Username:

Date/Password:

Date/Password:

Date/Password:

Date/Password:

Date/Password:

WEBSITE

Username:

Date/Password:

Date/Password:

Date/Password:

Date/Password:

Date/Password:

WEBSITE

Username:

Date/Password:

Date/Password:

Date/Password:

Date/Password:

Date/Password:

WEBSITE

Username:

Date/Password:

Date/Password:

Date/Password:

Date/Password:

Date/Password:

WEBSITE

Username:

Date/Password:

Date/Password:

Date/Password:

Date/Password:

Date/Password:

WEBSITE

Username:

Date/Password:

Date/Password:

Date/Password:

Date/Password:

Date/Password:

WEBSITE

Username:

Date/Password:

Date/Password:

Date/Password:

Date/Password:

Date/Password:

WEBSITE

Username:

Date/Password:

Date/Password:

Date/Password:

Date/Password:

Date/Password:

WEBSITE

Username:

Date/Password:

Date/Password:

Date/Password:

Date/Password:

Date/Password:

O
P

WEBSITE

Username:

Date/Password:

Date/Password:

Date/Password:

Date/Password:

Date/Password:

WEBSITE

Username:

Date/Password:

Date/Password:

Date/Password:

Date/Password:

Date/Password:

WEBSITE

Username:

Date/Password:

Date/Password:

Date/Password:

Date/Password:

Date/Password:

WEBSITE

Username:

Date/Password:

Date/Password:

Date/Password:

Date/Password:

Date/Password:

WEBSITE

Username:

Date/Password:

Date/Password:

Date/Password:

Date/Password:

Date/Password:

WEBSITE

Username:

Date/Password:

Date/Password:

Date/Password:

Date/Password:

Date/Password:

O
P

WEBSITE

Username:

Date/Password:

Date/Password:

Date/Password:

Date/Password:

Date/Password:

WEBSITE

Username:

Date/Password:

Date/Password:

Date/Password:

Date/Password:

Date/Password:

WEBSITE

Username:

Date/Password:

Date/Password:

Date/Password:

Date/Password:

Date/Password:

WEBSITE

Username:

Date/Password:

Date/Password:

Date/Password:

Date/Password:

Date/Password:

WEBSITE

Username:

Date/Password:

Date/Password:

Date/Password:

Date/Password:

Date/Password:

WEBSITE

Username:

Date/Password:

Date/Password:

Date/Password:

Date/Password:

Date/Password:

O
P

WEBSITE

Username:

Date/Password:

Date/Password:

Date/Password:

Date/Password:

Date/Password:

WEBSITE

Username:

Date/Password:

Date/Password:

Date/Password:

Date/Password:

Date/Password:

WEBSITE

Username:

Date/Password:

Date/Password:

Date/Password:

Date/Password:

Date/Password:

WEBSITE

Username:

Date/Password:

Date/Password:

Date/Password:

Date/Password:

Date/Password:

WEBSITE

Username:

Date/Password:

Date/Password:

Date/Password:

Date/Password:

Date/Password:

WEBSITE

Username:

Date/Password:

Date/Password:

Date/Password:

Date/Password:

Date/Password:

O
P

WEBSITE

Username:

Date/Password:

Date/Password:

Date/Password:

Date/Password:

Date/Password:

WEBSITE

Username:

Date/Password:

Date/Password:

Date/Password:

Date/Password:

Date/Password:

WEBSITE

Username:

Date/Password:

Date/Password:

Date/Password:

Date/Password:

Date/Password:

O
P

WEBSITE

Username:

Date/Password:

Date/Password:

Date/Password:

Date/Password:

Date/Password:

WEBSITE

Username:

Date/Password:

Date/Password:

Date/Password:

Date/Password:

Date/Password:

WEBSITE

Username:

Date/Password:

Date/Password:

Date/Password:

Date/Password:

Date/Password:

Q
R

tips   passwords   licenses   settings   notes

WEBSITE

Username:

Date/Password:

Date/Password:

Date/Password:

Date/Password:

Date/Password:

WEBSITE

Username:

Date/Password:

Date/Password:

Date/Password:

Date/Password:

Date/Password:

WEBSITE

Username:

Date/Password:

Date/Password:

Date/Password:

Date/Password:

Date/Password:

WEBSITE

Username:

Date/Password:

Date/Password:

Date/Password:

Date/Password:

Date/Password:

WEBSITE

Username:

Date/Password:

Date/Password:

Date/Password:

Date/Password:

Date/Password:

WEBSITE

Username:

Date/Password:

Date/Password:

Date/Password:

Date/Password:

Date/Password:

**Q
R**

WEBSITE

Username:

Date/Password:

Date/Password:

Date/Password:

Date/Password:

Date/Password:

WEBSITE

Username:

Date/Password:

Date/Password:

Date/Password:

Date/Password:

Date/Password:

WEBSITE

Username:

Date/Password:

Date/Password:

Date/Password:

Date/Password:

Date/Password:

WEBSITE

Username:

Date/Password:

Date/Password:

Date/Password:

Date/Password:

Date/Password:

WEBSITE

Username:

Date/Password:

Date/Password:

Date/Password:

Date/Password:

Date/Password:

WEBSITE

Username:

Date/Password:

Date/Password:

Date/Password:

Date/Password:

Date/Password:

Q
R

WEBSITE

Username:

Date/Password:

Date/Password:

Date/Password:

Date/Password:

Date/Password:

WEBSITE

Username:

Date/Password:

Date/Password:

Date/Password:

Date/Password:

Date/Password:

WEBSITE

Username:

Date/Password:

Date/Password:

Date/Password:

Date/Password:

Date/Password:

WEBSITE

Username:

Date/Password:

Date/Password:

Date/Password:

Date/Password:

Date/Password:

WEBSITE

Username:

Date/Password:

Date/Password:

Date/Password:

Date/Password:

Date/Password:

WEBSITE

Username:

Date/Password:

Date/Password:

Date/Password:

Date/Password:

Date/Password:

WEBSITE

Username:

Date/Password:

Date/Password:

Date/Password:

Date/Password:

Date/Password:

WEBSITE

Username:

Date/Password:

Date/Password:

Date/Password:

Date/Password:

Date/Password:

WEBSITE

Username:

Date/Password:

Date/Password:

Date/Password:

Date/Password:

Date/Password:

WEBSITE

Username:

Date/Password:

Date/Password:

Date/Password:

Date/Password:

Date/Password:

WEBSITE

Username:

Date/Password:

Date/Password:

Date/Password:

Date/Password:

Date/Password:

WEBSITE

Username:

Date/Password:

Date/Password:

Date/Password:

Date/Password:

Date/Password:

S
T

WEBSITE

Username:

Date/Password:

Date/Password:

Date/Password:

Date/Password:

Date/Password:

WEBSITE

Username:

Date/Password:

Date/Password:

Date/Password:

Date/Password:

Date/Password:

WEBSITE

Username:

Date/Password:

Date/Password:

Date/Password:

Date/Password:

Date/Password:

WEBSITE

Username:

Date/Password:

Date/Password:

Date/Password:

Date/Password:

Date/Password:

WEBSITE

Username:

Date/Password:

Date/Password:

Date/Password:

Date/Password:

Date/Password:

WEBSITE

Username:

Date/Password:

Date/Password:

Date/Password:

Date/Password:

Date/Password:

S
T

WEBSITE

Username:

Date/Password:

Date/Password:

Date/Password:

Date/Password:

Date/Password:

WEBSITE

Username:

Date/Password:

Date/Password:

Date/Password:

Date/Password:

Date/Password:

WEBSITE

Username:

Date/Password:

Date/Password:

Date/Password:

Date/Password:

Date/Password:

WEBSITE

Username:

Date/Password:

Date/Password:

Date/Password:

Date/Password:

Date/Password:

WEBSITE

Username:

Date/Password:

Date/Password:

Date/Password:

Date/Password:

Date/Password:

WEBSITE

Username:

Date/Password:

Date/Password:

Date/Password:

Date/Password:

Date/Password:

S
T

WEBSITE

Username:

Date/Password:

Date/Password:

Date/Password:

Date/Password:

Date/Password:

WEBSITE

Username:

Date/Password:

Date/Password:

Date/Password:

Date/Password:

Date/Password:

WEBSITE

Username:

Date/Password:

Date/Password:

Date/Password:

Date/Password:

Date/Password:

WEBSITE

Username:

Date/Password:

Date/Password:

Date/Password:

Date/Password:

Date/Password:

WEBSITE

Username:

Date/Password:

Date/Password:

Date/Password:

Date/Password:

Date/Password:

WEBSITE

Username:

Date/Password:

Date/Password:

Date/Password:

Date/Password:

Date/Password:

S
T

WEBSITE

Username:

Date/Password:

Date/Password:

Date/Password:

Date/Password:

Date/Password:

WEBSITE

Username:

Date/Password:

Date/Password:

Date/Password:

Date/Password:

Date/Password:

WEBSITE

Username:

Date/Password:

Date/Password:

Date/Password:

Date/Password:

Date/Password:

WEBSITE

Username:

Date/Password:

Date/Password:

Date/Password:

Date/Password:

Date/Password:

WEBSITE

Username:

Date/Password:

Date/Password:

Date/Password:

Date/Password:

Date/Password:

WEBSITE

Username:

Date/Password:

Date/Password:

Date/Password:

Date/Password:

Date/Password:

U
V

WEBSITE

Username:

Date/Password:

Date/Password:

Date/Password:

Date/Password:

Date/Password:

WEBSITE

Username:

Date/Password:

Date/Password:

Date/Password:

Date/Password:

Date/Password:

WEBSITE

Username:

Date/Password:

Date/Password:

Date/Password:

Date/Password:

Date/Password:

WEBSITE

Username:

Date/Password:

Date/Password:

Date/Password:

Date/Password:

Date/Password:

WEBSITE

Username:

Date/Password:

Date/Password:

Date/Password:

Date/Password:

Date/Password:

WEBSITE

Username:

Date/Password:

Date/Password:

Date/Password:

Date/Password:

Date/Password:

WEBSITE

Username:

Date/Password:

Date/Password:

Date/Password:

Date/Password:

Date/Password:

WEBSITE

Username:

Date/Password:

Date/Password:

Date/Password:

Date/Password:

Date/Password:

WEBSITE

Username:

Date/Password:

Date/Password:

Date/Password:

Date/Password:

Date/Password:

WEBSITE

Username:

Date/Password:

Date/Password:

Date/Password:

Date/Password:

Date/Password:

WEBSITE

Username:

Date/Password:

Date/Password:

Date/Password:

Date/Password:

Date/Password:

WEBSITE

Username:

Date/Password:

Date/Password:

Date/Password:

Date/Password:

Date/Password:

U
V

WEBSITE

Username:

Date/Password:

Date/Password:

Date/Password:

Date/Password:

Date/Password:

WEBSITE

Username:

Date/Password:

Date/Password:

Date/Password:

Date/Password:

Date/Password:

WEBSITE

Username:

Date/Password:

Date/Password:

Date/Password:

Date/Password:

Date/Password:

WEBSITE

Username:

Date/Password:

Date/Password:

Date/Password:

Date/Password:

Date/Password:

WEBSITE

Username:

Date/Password:

Date/Password:

Date/Password:

Date/Password:

Date/Password:

WEBSITE

Username:

Date/Password:

Date/Password:

Date/Password:

Date/Password:

Date/Password:

U
V

WEBSITE

Username:

Date/Password:

Date/Password:

Date/Password:

Date/Password:

Date/Password:

WEBSITE

Username:

Date/Password:

Date/Password:

Date/Password:

Date/Password:

Date/Password:

WEBSITE

Username:

Date/Password:

Date/Password:

Date/Password:

Date/Password:

Date/Password:

U
V

WEBSITE

Username:

Date/Password:

Date/Password:

Date/Password:

Date/Password:

Date/Password:

WEBSITE

Username:

Date/Password:

Date/Password:

Date/Password:

Date/Password:

Date/Password:

WEBSITE

Username:

Date/Password:

Date/Password:

Date/Password:

Date/Password:

Date/Password:

W
X

WEBSITE

Username:

Date/Password:

Date/Password:

Date/Password:

Date/Password:

Date/Password:

WEBSITE

Username:

Date/Password:

Date/Password:

Date/Password:

Date/Password:

Date/Password:

WEBSITE

Username:

Date/Password:

Date/Password:

Date/Password:

Date/Password:

Date/Password:

WEBSITE

Username:

Date/Password:

Date/Password:

Date/Password:

Date/Password:

Date/Password:

WEBSITE

Username:

Date/Password:

Date/Password:

Date/Password:

Date/Password:

Date/Password:

WEBSITE

Username:

Date/Password:

Date/Password:

Date/Password:

Date/Password:

Date/Password:

W
X

WEBSITE

Username:

Date/Password:

Date/Password:

Date/Password:

Date/Password:

Date/Password:

WEBSITE

Username:

Date/Password:

Date/Password:

Date/Password:

Date/Password:

Date/Password:

WEBSITE

Username:

Date/Password:

Date/Password:

Date/Password:

Date/Password:

Date/Password:

W
X

WEBSITE

Username:

Date/Password:

Date/Password:

Date/Password:

Date/Password:

Date/Password:

WEBSITE

Username:

Date/Password:

Date/Password:

Date/Password:

Date/Password:

Date/Password:

WEBSITE

Username:

Date/Password:

Date/Password:

Date/Password:

Date/Password:

Date/Password:

W
X

WEBSITE

Username:

Date/Password:

Date/Password:

Date/Password:

Date/Password:

Date/Password:

WEBSITE

Username:

Date/Password:

Date/Password:

Date/Password:

Date/Password:

Date/Password:

WEBSITE

Username:

Date/Password:

Date/Password:

Date/Password:

Date/Password:

Date/Password:

W
X

WEBSITE

Username:

Date/Password:

Date/Password:

Date/Password:

Date/Password:

Date/Password:

WEBSITE

Username:

Date/Password:

Date/Password:

Date/Password:

Date/Password:

Date/Password:

WEBSITE

Username:

Date/Password:

Date/Password:

Date/Password:

Date/Password:

Date/Password:

W
X

WEBSITE

Username:

Date/Password:

Date/Password:

Date/Password:

Date/Password:

Date/Password:

WEBSITE

Username:

Date/Password:

Date/Password:

Date/Password:

Date/Password:

Date/Password:

WEBSITE

Username:

Date/Password:

Date/Password:

Date/Password:

Date/Password:

Date/Password:

WEBSITE

Username:

Date/Password:

Date/Password:

Date/Password:

Date/Password:

Date/Password:

WEBSITE

Username:

Date/Password:

Date/Password:

Date/Password:

Date/Password:

Date/Password:

WEBSITE

Username:

Date/Password:

Date/Password:

Date/Password:

Date/Password:

Date/Password:

WEBSITE

Username:

Date/Password:

Date/Password:

Date/Password:

Date/Password:

Date/Password:

WEBSITE

Username:

Date/Password:

Date/Password:

Date/Password:

Date/Password:

Date/Password:

WEBSITE

Username:

Date/Password:

Date/Password:

Date/Password:

Date/Password:

Date/Password:

WEBSITE

Username:

Date/Password:

Date/Password:

Date/Password:

Date/Password:

Date/Password:

WEBSITE

Username:

Date/Password:

Date/Password:

Date/Password:

Date/Password:

Date/Password:

WEBSITE

Username:

Date/Password:

Date/Password:

Date/Password:

Date/Password:

Date/Password:

WEBSITE

Username:

Date/Password:

Date/Password:

Date/Password:

Date/Password:

Date/Password:

WEBSITE

Username:

Date/Password:

Date/Password:

Date/Password:

Date/Password:

Date/Password:

WEBSITE

Username:

Date/Password:

Date/Password:

Date/Password:

Date/Password:

Date/Password:

Y
Z

WEBSITE

Username:

Date/Password:

Date/Password:

Date/Password:

Date/Password:

Date/Password:

WEBSITE

Username:

Date/Password:

Date/Password:

Date/Password:

Date/Password:

Date/Password:

WEBSITE

Username:

Date/Password:

Date/Password:

Date/Password:

Date/Password:

Date/Password:

WEBSITE

Username:

Date/Password:

Date/Password:

Date/Password:

Date/Password:

Date/Password:

WEBSITE

Username:

Date/Password:

Date/Password:

Date/Password:

Date/Password:

Date/Password:

WEBSITE

Username:

Date/Password:

Date/Password:

Date/Password:

Date/Password:

Date/Password:

WEBSITE

Username:

Date/Password:

Date/Password:

Date/Password:

Date/Password:

Date/Password:

WEBSITE

Username:

Date/Password:

Date/Password:

Date/Password:

Date/Password:

Date/Password:

WEBSITE

Username:

Date/Password:

Date/Password:

Date/Password:

Date/Password:

Date/Password:

WEBSITE

Username:

Date/Password:

Date/Password:

Date/Password:

Date/Password:

Date/Password:

WEBSITE

Username:

Date/Password:

Date/Password:

Date/Password:

Date/Password:

Date/Password:

WEBSITE

Username:

Date/Password:

Date/Password:

Date/Password:

Date/Password:

Date/Password:

Y
Z

SOFTWARE

License Number:

Purchase Date:

Subscription License Renewal Date:

Monthly Fee:

SOFTWARE

License Number:

Purchase Date:

Subscription License Renewal Date:

Monthly Fee:

SOFTWARE

License Number:

Purchase Date:

Subscription License Renewal Date:

Monthly Fee:

SOFTWARE

License Number:

Purchase Date:

Subscription License Renewal Date:

Monthly Fee:

SOFTWARE

License Number:

Purchase Date:

Subscription License Renewal Date:

Monthly Fee:

SOFTWARE

License Number:

Purchase Date:

Subscription License Renewal Date:

Monthly Fee:

SOFTWARE

License Number:

Purchase Date:

Subscription License Renewal Date:

Monthly Fee:

SOFTWARE

License Number:

Purchase Date:

Subscription License Renewal Date:

Monthly Fee:

SOFTWARE

License Number:

Purchase Date:

Subscription License Renewal Date:

Monthly Fee:

SOFTWARE

License Number:

Purchase Date:

Subscription License Renewal Date:

Monthly Fee:

SOFTWARE

License Number:

Purchase Date:

Subscription License Renewal Date:

Monthly Fee:

SOFTWARE

License Number:

Purchase Date:

Subscription License Renewal Date:

Monthly Fee:

SOFTWARE

License Number:

Purchase Date:

Subscription License Renewal Date:

Monthly Fee:

SOFTWARE

License Number:

Purchase Date:

Subscription License Renewal Date:

Monthly Fee:

SOFTWARE

License Number:

Purchase Date:

Subscription License Renewal Date:

Monthly Fee:

SOFTWARE

License Number:

Purchase Date:

Subscription License Renewal Date:

Monthly Fee:

SOFTWARE

License Number:

Purchase Date:

Subscription License Renewal Date:

Monthly Fee:

SOFTWARE

License Number:

Purchase Date:

Subscription License Renewal Date:

Monthly Fee:

SOFTWARE

License Number:

Purchase Date:

Subscription License Renewal Date:

Monthly Fee:

SOFTWARE

License Number:

Purchase Date:

Subscription License Renewal Date:

Monthly Fee:

SOFTWARE

License Number:

Purchase Date:

Subscription License Renewal Date:

Monthly Fee:

SOFTWARE

License Number:

Purchase Date:

Subscription License Renewal Date:

Monthly Fee:

SOFTWARE

License Number:

Purchase Date:

Subscription License Renewal Date:

Monthly Fee:

SOFTWARE

License Number:

Purchase Date:

Subscription License Renewal Date:

Monthly Fee:

BROADBAND MODEM

Model:

Serial #:

Mac Address:

Administration URL/IP Address:

WAN IP Address:

Username:

Date/Password:

Date/Password:

Date/Password:

Date/Password:

ROUTER/WIRELESS ACCESS POINT

Model:

Serial #:

Factory Default Admin IP Address:

Factory Default Username:

Factory Default Password:

User Defined Admin URL/IP Address:

User Defined Username:

User Defined Password/Date:

BROADBAND MODEM

Model:

Serial #:

Mac Address:

Administration URL/IP Address:

WAN IP Address:

Username:

Date/Password:

Date/Password:

Date/Password:

Date/Password:

ROUTER/WIRELESS ACCESS POINT

Model:

Serial #:

Factory Default Admin IP Address:

Factory Default Username:

Factory Default Password:

User Defined Admin URL/IP Address:

User Defined Username:

User Defined Password/Date:

BROADBAND MODEM

Model:

Serial #:

Mac Address:

Administration URL/IP Address:

WAN IP Address:

Username:

Date/Password:

Date/Password:

Date/Password:

Date/Password:

ROUTER/WIRELESS ACCESS POINT

Model:

Serial #:

Factory Default Admin IP Address:

Factory Default Username:

Factory Default Password:

User Defined Admin URL/IP Address:

User Defined Username:

User Defined Password/Date:

WAN SETTINGS

MAC Address (see Broadband Modem):

IP Address (see Broadband Modem):

Host Name (if required by ISP):

Domain Name (if required by ISP):

Subnet Mask:

Default Gateway:

DNS—Primary:

DNS—Secondary:

LAN SETTINGS

IP Address:

Subnet Mask:

DHCP Range (if DHCP enabled):

WIRELESS SETTINGS

SSID (Wireless Network Name):

Channel:

Security Mode:

Shared Key (for WPA):

Passphrase (for WEP):

WAN SETTINGS

MAC Address (see Broadband Modem):

IP Address (see Broadband Modem):

Host Name (if required by ISP):

Domain Name (if required by ISP):

Subnet Mask:

Default Gateway:

DNS—Primary:

DNS—Secondary:

LAN SETTINGS

IP Address:

Subnet Mask:

DHCP Range (if DHCP enabled):

WIRELESS SETTINGS

SSID (Wireless Network Name):

Channel:

Security Mode:

Shared Key (for WPA):

Passphrase (for WEP):

WAN SETTINGS

MAC Address (see Broadband Modem):

IP Address (see Broadband Modem):

Host Name (if required by ISP):

Domain Name (if required by ISP):

Subnet Mask:

Default Gateway:

DNS—Primary:

DNS—Secondary:

LAN SETTINGS

IP Address:

Subnet Mask:

DHCP Range (if DHCP enabled):

WIRELESS SETTINGS

SSID (Wireless Network Name):

Channel:

Security Mode:

Shared Key (for WPA):

Passphrase (for WEP):

NOTES

NOTES

NOTES

NOTES